BAD GUYS

SWINDLERS

BAD GUYS

SWINDLERS

by Gary L. Blackwood

BENCHMARK BOOKS

MARSHALL CAVENDISH
NEW YORK

Benchmark Books
Marshall Cavendish Corporation
99 White Plains Road
Tarrytown, New York 10591-9001
Website: www.marshallcavendish.com

———◆———

Library of Congress Cataloging-in-Publication Data

Blackwood, Gary L.
Swindlers / by Gary L. Blackwood
p.cm. – (Bad guys ; 3)
Includes bibliographical references (p. 69) and index.
ISBN 0-7614-1031-7 (lib. bdg.)
1. Swindlers and swindling—History—Juvenile literature. 2. Swindlers and swindling—Biography—
Juvenile literature. [1. Swindlers and swindling.] I. Title. II. Series: Blackwood, Gary L. Bad guys ; 3.
HV6691.B478 2001   364.16'3—dc21   00-057153

Book Design by Gysela Pacheco

Picture Research by Linda Sykes Picture Research, Hilton Head SC

Front cover: Stock Montage; page 1: Hulton-Deutsch/Corbis; pages 10,
24, 28: Culver Pictures; pages 2-3,12, 16, 30, 33, 36, 39, 42, 45, 46:
Corbis-Bettmann; page 19: Alaska State Library, Juneau; page 21:The
Huntington Library; pages 48, 56, 65: AP/Wide World; page 53: George
Rodger/TimePix; page 54: Yale Joel/TimePix; page 55:
UPI/Corbis-Bettmann; page 60: Lake County/Corbis.

Printed in Italy

1 3 5 6 4 2

On the cover and title page: *Most sorts of swindlers rely on their intelligence
and charm. But some scams, like the phony coins being created by counterfeiters
in the nineteenth century, demand practical skills, such as engraving and metal
casting.*

Contents

Introduction 6

One   The Shakespeare Scam   9

Two   King of the Thimbleriggers   17

Three   The Queen of Confidence Women   25

Four   The Yellow Kid   32

Five   The Greatest Faker   41

Six   The True Con Artist   49

Seven   The Great Impostor   57

Glossary   66

To Learn More about Swindlers   68

Bibliography   69

Index   71

Introduction

In April 2000, as part of an investigation called Operation Bullpen, federal agents arrested twenty members of a Southern California forgery ring. The ring specialized in selling items they claimed had been personally autographed by celebrities ranging from Abraham Lincoln to Mark McGwire. Among their more outrageous forgeries was a baseball supposedly signed by Mother Teresa.

For every swindle like this that makes the news, there are hundreds of others that go unreported and unpunished. Fraud, fakery, and forgery are so rampant, in fact, that scholar Ralph Hancock believes "the art of deception is practiced today by more people in more ways for more profit than ever before in the history of the world."

But swindling—using fraudulent means to obtain money, property, or something else of value—is certainly not a modern invention. Indeed, it's one of the oldest crimes on record. Swindlers fall into three basic types—the impostor, the forger, and the confidence artist—and all three have been around since the beginnings of humankind.

One of the earliest stories in the Bible is the tale of an impostor, Jacob, who fraudulently obtains his blind

Swindlers are often motivated by something besides money. "How tiresome it is," declares the forger in Thomas Mann's story "Felix Krull," "to sign all one's life long the same name to letters and papers!"

father's blessing by donning goatskins and impersonating his hairy brother, Esau.

In the sixth century B.C., Onomacritus, a Greek fortune-teller known as the Father of Fakers, showed a knack for eliciting from the gods prophecies that pleased his clients, the tyrants Pisistratus and Hipparchus. His success was, of course, due to the fact that he composed the messages himself. When his forgeries were discovered, he was banished.

Though the term "confidence trick" wasn't widely used until Herman Melville's novel *The Confidence Man* appeared in 1857, con artists have been operating for ages. The well-known shell game, in which the victim tries to choose which of three shells conceals a pea, probably got its start in Greece some two thousand years ago; its practitioners used stones and seashells.

The general public—with the exception of the victims, of course—has always regarded such shady activities as something less than full-fledged crimes. In fact, people often seem to actually admire a successful swindler. In hundreds of folktales and stories, from *The Arabian Nights* to Shakespeare's plays to the motion picture *The Sting*, characters who succeed through the use of trickery or deceit are presented as heroes.

Of course literature and public opinion have also made heroes out of the likes of John Dillinger, Dick Turpin, and Billy the Kid. Though the swindler is no less of a thief than the Wild West outlaw, the gangster, or the highwayman, most do have one redeeming virtue: they shun violence. Rather than using a weapon to get what they want, they prefer to use their wits.

One
The Shakespeare Scam

Many swindlers have skills and talents that would surely have brought them success in a legitimate line of work. Among the most talented are the literary forgers.

Writers have been passing off their work as someone else's almost since written language was invented. The art undoubtedly reached its peak, though, in the 1700s and 1800s. According to author John Whitehead, "Literary forgery seemed to be so easy and attractive . . . that a good number of people succumbed to the temptation." Among them were such noted authors as Daniel Defoe, Benjamin Franklin, and poet James Whitcomb Riley.

Defoe's *A Journal of the Plague Year* claimed to be an eyewitness account of the plague of 1665, "Written by a Citizen who continued all the while in London"— specifically a saddle maker identified only by the initials "H. F." Since Defoe was only five in 1665, most scholars believe he drew on official records, interviews with plague survivors, and his own imagination.

Franklin penned a number of fakes, including a speech supposedly made by a female convict, arguing for equal rights for women under the law, a news story about a witchcraft trial that never occurred, and a previously unknown chapter of the Bible's Book of Genesis.

Writing about literary forgers, English author John Whitehead boasts, "The British have always appeared to be the masters in this particular line of deceit." Eighteenth-century poet Thomas Chatterton was one of the most gifted.

In his poem "Leonainie," Riley imitated the literary style and the handwriting of Edgar Allen Poe and even signed the poem "E. A. P." When Riley later confessed that he was the poem's author, one critic indignantly accused him of trying to pass off Poe's work as his own.

The sophisticated scientific techniques now used to determine authenticity—X-raying and chemical analysis, for example—hadn't been invented yet, so a forger who was clever enough could fool even the experts. Thomas Chatterton wasn't quite clever enough.

Chatterton was born in Bristol, England, in 1752. By the time he was sixteen he was showing extraordinary promise as a poet. But instead of taking credit for his work, he ascribed it to a fifteenth-century monk named Thomas Rowley, apparently thinking it would attract more notice. Chatterton sent several pieces to the popular novelist Horace Walpole, who believed them genuine. But two of Walpole's friends, both poets, denounced them as fakes. At the age of seventeen, destitute and disillusioned, Chatterton swallowed a lethal dose of rat poison.

Two decades after his death, Chatterton's brief foray into forgery inspired another teenage boy to embark on a far more audacious and far more successful scheme.

William Henry Ireland was born in 1777 the son of a respected London bookseller, artist, and Shakespeare enthusiast named Samuel Ireland. A poor student, William bounced around from school to school, finishing up his spotty education with a three-year stay in France.

On his return to England, around 1793, he apprenticed to a conveyancer, a lawyer who specialized in

Like most swindlers, William Henry Ireland placed much of the blame on the people he duped. "It is extraordinary to observe," he wrote, "how willingly persons will blind themselves on any point interesting to their feelings."

drawing up deeds and examining property titles. In his off hours William shared his father's interest in Shakespeare. They visited the bard's birthplace at Stratford-upon-Avon, where Samuel purchased some mementoes of questionable origin, including a purse and a chair that supposedly once belonged to Shakespeare's wife, Anne Hathaway.

At about the same time, William became fascinated with Thomas Chatterton's short-lived career, especially the forgeries. Gradually he began planning a scam of his own. His first step was to make tracings of two authentic Shakespeare autographs. Next he secretly cut pieces of parchment from the century-old papers in the conveyancer's files. A friend in a printer's shop helped him concoct a type of ink that gave the appearance of age.

Armed with these tools, plus a familiarity with the outdated English used in old documents, William created a phony deed to which he appended a facsimile of Shakespeare's signature. He showed the deed to his father, explaining that he had come across it among some old papers belonging to an unnamed "gentleman of fortune."

Samuel Ireland was astounded, but accepted the document as genuine. So did his literary friends. Delighted that his maiden effort had been so well received, the boy composed a three-hundred-word "Profession of Faith by William Shakespeare," which was also declared authentic by experts. William topped this triumph by "discovering" not only extracts from the original script of *Hamlet* but also a box containing a lock of the bard's hair!

The collection drew a host of admirers, including the Prince of Wales and diarist-biographer James Boswell, who was so awed that he asked to be allowed to kiss "the invaluable relics of our bard." William went on to unearth a seemingly endless supply of Shakespeariana, including love letters addressed to Anne Hathaway and a note from Queen Elizabeth I, complimenting the playwright on his "prettye verses." Though they resembled a bad parody of sixteenth-century grammar and spelling, all were accepted as the real thing.

Intoxicated by his success, William conceived a forgery that would overshadow all the others—and would prove to be his undoing: a complete, previously unknown Shakespeare play. William's inspiration came from a drawing his father had done of Vortigern, the Welsh warrior king, and his queen, Rowena.

Before he had written a word, he impulsively described the nonexistent play to his father. With the elder Ireland continually demanding to see the script, William set to work. He later wrote, "I was really so unacquainted with the proper length of a drama as to be compelled to count the number of lines in one of Shakespeare's plays." Unfortunately the play he chose to emulate was unusually long. Nevertheless, he managed to turn out *Vortigern and Rowena* in a mere two months.

The play was hardly up to Shakespeare's standards, but, considering the author's age and the speed with which he wrote it, *Vortigern* was an impressive effort. Playwright Richard Brinsley Sheridan promptly bought the rights to produce the drama at London's famed Drury Lane Theatre, and paid William an advance of sixty pounds.

Vortigern and Rowena opened on April 2, 1796, to a

sold-out crowd. But the cast was not nearly as enthusiastic about the play as Sheridan was. The celebrated actor John Kemble, who played the lead, considered it a travesty, one that should rightly have been presented a day earlier—on April Fools' Day. He and his fellow performers hammed it up so outrageously that the audience, probably spurred on by associates Kemble had planted among them, began laughing and jeering.

Despite the dismal failure of *Vortigern,* William proceeded with plans to compose a whole series of lost Shakespeare plays, and managed to complete one titled *Henry II* before the accusations of fakery became too loud and numerous to ignore.

Since William was considered too young to have pulled off such a feat, the burden of suspicion fell on Samuel Ireland. Anxious to "clear my father's character from the odium which was so unjustly heaped upon it," William finally admitted his guilt. But Samuel refused to believe that the letters and plays were fakes. He assumed instead that his son's confession was the fake, a noble attempt to spare his father from further attacks.

The scandal severely damaged William's chances for a legitimate literary career. Though *Henry II* was a stronger play than *Vortigern,* no theater would touch it. For a time William eked out a living as a book dealer and copyist, supplementing his income by selling copies of his famous forgeries. He went on writing, often using a pen name, and eventually had a number of poems and novels published. He even tried his hand at the occasional play.

Not content with writing phony plays, William branched out into art forgery with this crude "self-portrait" of Shakespeare, complete with autographs.

But he never quite managed to put his youthful follies behind him. In 1805 he published a lengthy "Confession" in which he pointed out that the critics who had accepted the forgeries were as much to blame as he was. A few years before his death he brought out a new edition of *Vortigern and Rowena*. In the preface he protested the "shafts of persecution relentlessly levelled against me for upwards of thirty years." By that time, though, the whole affair was largely forgotten, and when William Ireland died in 1835, hardly anyone took note of his passing.

Two

King of the Thimbleriggers

As the heyday of the literary forger came to a close, another sort of swindler was waiting in the wings, ready to take center stage—the confidence artist.

In the last half of the nineteenth century a series of mining booms rocked the American West, beginning with the California gold rush in 1849. The wild and lawless mining towns attracted droves of men and women seeking their fortune, and close behind came a contingent of criminals intent on relieving them of it.

One of the most successful was a complex character known as Soapy Smith. Though he was a consummate con man, Soapy aspired to something more. In his desire for power and his simultaneous longing for respectability, he resembled the great gang bosses, such as Paul Kelly and Al Capone, who ruled New York and Chicago in the early decades of the twentieth century (see *Gangsters* in this series).

Soapy was born Jefferson Randolph Smith in 1860. Growing up in Georgia, he acquired the soft drawl, tasteful attire, and cultured manner of a Southern gentleman—qualities that inspired trust in his victims.

He started out on the straight and narrow path,

studying to be a Baptist minister. Sometime in his twenties, though, he got an itch for adventure and headed west, where he worked as a cowhand, driving longhorns north from Texas on the Chisholm Trail. At the end of one cattle drive he encountered a con man who was fleecing victims with the old shell game. Smith proceeded to lose a month's wages to the man. The experience taught him a valuable lesson—that he could make a lot more money with a lot less work.

Smith apprenticed himself to the con man and, once he had learned the tricks of the trade, set out on his own. In the silver mining town of Leadville, Colorado, he perfected the scam that was the source of his nickname.

Setting up a table on a street corner, he called to passersby, "Come gentlemen, cleanliness is next to godliness; buy a cake of soap for the richest bath you ever had. Five dollars can get you one hundred!" Meanwhile, his deft hands were wrapping bars of soap in twenty, fifty, and one hundred dollar bills—or so it seemed. When a crowd had gathered, an accomplice of Smith's stepped forward, bought a cake of soap, and unwrapped it, revealing a one hundred dollar bill. Unfortunately those who eagerly followed suit found nothing under the wrapper but a five-cent cake of soap.

Soapy moved on to Denver, where he recruited fellow grifters into a regular corporation of crime. The "Soap Gang" organized phony lotteries, rigged prize fights, and operated a gambling hall. Soapy's many successful cons earned him the title King of the Thimbleriggers—another term for a swindler.

Despite his criminal activities, Soapy Smith (center) always considered himself an advocate of law and order—as long as he was the one making the laws and giving the orders.

In 1892 the Soap Gang's supremacy was threatened by another gang. When the rivalry turned into open warfare, the public demanded a citywide cleanup of crime, and Soapy looked for a new base of operations.

He chose the wide-open mining camp of Creede, run by a saloon owner named Bob Ford—the "dirty little coward" who, ten years earlier, had shot down Jesse James (see *Outlaws* in this series).

When Soapy began running his old reliable soap scam, Ford ordered him out of town. But instead of leaving, Soapy smooth-talked his way into a partnership with Ford. Their first scheme showcased Soapy's imaginative streak and his sense of humor.

Back in Denver he'd come upon a lifelike human figure made of cement and plaster. He had the statue shipped to Creede and half-buried in a canyon, where a prospector mistook it for a petrified body. Soapy put the figure on display at Ford's saloon and charged crowds of curious townsfolk twenty-five cents each to view what his handbills touted as "The Missing Link! See him in the flesh (petrified) and hear his anatomy and life story described in all its particulars by Professor Jefferson Randolph Smith! (Ladies will not be admitted.)"

In June, Ford was gunned down by the brother-in-law of two James Gang members, and Soapy became the sole boss of Creede. But a movement was under way to bring law and order to the town and, rather than fight it, Soapy again moved on. After being run out of St. Louis and Houston, he drifted into Mexico. Posing as an army colonel, he convinced Mexican president Porfirio Díaz that he could raise a force of American mercenaries to subdue the country's rebellious peasants. Díaz forked over four thousand pesos before he discovered the true identity of the "colonel."

Soapy returned to Denver and opened a lavish—and crooked—gambling hall. When two irate victims took him to court, Soapy argued that "when a man goes broke at one of my tables he's learned a lesson he'll never forget. I am therefore providing a valuable and moral community service." The case was dismissed.

During his absence the ruthless Blonger brothers had taken control of the Denver underworld, and Soapy was reluctant to challenge them. When news of a gold strike in Canada's Klondike region reached Denver in the summer of 1897, Soapy headed north, taking with him five trusted henchmen. By October they were busy fleecing the *cheechakos* (newcomers) who passed through

In the late 1880s, Denver was an ideal location for con men. As long as they preyed only on strangers and left the locals alone, city officials didn't bother them. In fact, the authorities often enlisted their help in rigging elections.

the Alaskan port of Skagway on their way to the goldfields.

Soon Skagway was overrun with legitimate-looking enterprises—a merchant's exchange, an information bureau, a ticket office, a freight company—that were really in the business of luring in victims to be mugged by Soapy's growing gang. The telegraph office offered a more subtle variation. For five dollars miners could send a message anywhere in the world and receive—collect, of course—a reply that was prompt but phony, since no telegraph lines linked Skagway to the outside world.

Early in 1898, sailors who had put in at Skagway reported that "Soapy Smith and his gang are in full control. Law-abiding people do not dare say a word against them. Holdups, robberies and shootings are part of the routine."

Though Soapy personally shunned violence, the members of his gang seldom hesitated to beat into submission or even shoot an uncooperative victim. As the violence escalated, alarmed citizens formed a vigilante group, the Committee of 101, and posted a notice ordering "all con men, bunco and sure-thing men and all other objectionable characters" to leave town.

Soapy countered by forming the Committee of Law and Order, which warned the vigilantes not to take the law into their own hands. Surprisingly, many towns-people sided with Soapy, who had carefully cultivated an image as the town's protector and benefactor, partly by controlling what the newspapers said about him and partly by performing very visible acts of charity.

To deal with the packs of abandoned sled dogs that roamed the streets, he launched an adopt-a-dog program, and took in six strays himself. He raised money to aid the widows of dead miners and to assist penniless prospectors—many of whom had lost their money to Soapy's gang. Such displays of generosity moved one reporter to call Soapy "the most gracious, kind hearted man I've ever met."

At some point Soapy began to believe his own press, and to relish the praise his good deeds brought him. "Wealth and power were no longer enough for him," writes historian Pierre Berton. "He wanted homage. . . . he craved the devotion of the entire community." But he wasn't willing to give up his criminal pursuits in order to get it.

In July 1898, successful miners began returning from the goldfields. Soapy's men waylaid one and relieved him of $2,800 in gold dust. The victim complained so loudly and incessantly that local merchants feared it would cause other rich prospectors to avoid their town.

The Committee of 101 gathered to address the problem. They met on one of the shipping docks, where Soapy's spies couldn't eavesdrop. Resentful of the growing sentiment against him, Soapy had begun drinking heavily. Despite his distaste for violence, he decided it was time for a showdown. Armed with a Winchester rifle, he headed for the docks.

A vigilante named Frank Reid blocked his way. Reid pushed the Winchester aside and drew a revolver, but

The Klondike gold rush attracted tens of thousands of people determined to "get rich quick." The ones who usually succeeded were not the prospectors, but the con men—and the legitimate merchants—who took their money.

the gun misfired. Soapy fired twice with the rifle, mortally wounding Reid. But the man managed to pull off a shot that struck Soapy in the heart. So ended Jefferson Randolph Smith's career as King of the Thimbleriggers. He was thirty-eight years old.

Three

The Queen of Confidence Women

Not many swindlers come to the sort of violent end that awaited Soapy Smith. In a few isolated cases, irate citizens have strung up a fellow who fleeced them once too often. For example, in Vicksburg, Mississippi, in 1835, a vigilante group known as the Volunteers hanged a gambler named John North and four of his associates.

But the cleverest grifters were seldom caught, partly because they covered their tracks so well and partly because, as master con man Joseph Weil put it, most victims "preferred to take their losses rather than let the world know that they had been so gullible."

When the law did manage to catch a con artist, the punishment was often relatively mild. But even those who received a lengthy prison sentence usually emerged unremorseful and unreformed. Ellen Peck, dubbed the "queen of confidence women" by the New York police, served at least four jail terms, yet she invariably returned at once to her wicked ways.

Peck's career was probably longer than that of any other con woman in history—an amazing feat, considering she didn't begin a life of crime until she was over fifty. When she was born in 1829 in Woodville, New

Hampshire, her name was Nellie Crosby. Her early life was mostly uneventful. For a time she taught school in Connecticut, then moved to New York City, where her elegant beauty attracted a businessman named Richard W. Peck. They married and settled down in Sparkville, New York, and for the next twenty-five years or so Mrs. Peck performed the traditional wifely duties of raising children and keeping house.

Then around 1880, apparently dissatisfied with domestic life, she abruptly left home and took up residence at a hotel in New York City—a daring move for a woman in those conservative times. In her outward appearance, though, Peck was quite respectable— "demure in manner and faultless in face and form," according to one description. She had a "neat and quiet way of dressing and ladylike manner."

At a social gathering she arranged to be introduced to B. T. Babbit, an elderly millionaire, and charmed her way into his confidence. For a man who had made a fortune in the business world, Babbit was remarkably gullible and trusting. Peck visited him frequently at his office and, if he was called away for some reason, he blithely let her stay. She took advantage of the opportunity to rummage through his desk drawers. One day she came upon a portfolio containing ten thousand dollars' worth of negotiable bonds. She spirited them away beneath her dress and sold them.

Babbit was distraught by the loss, but never suspected his lovely lady friend. When she brazenly offered to investigate the theft, he actually agreed, and wrote out a check for five thousand dollars to cover her expenses. Not surprisingly, the "case" dragged on so long that Peck was obliged to ask for another five thousand, which Babbit readily gave her.

The millionaire went on trusting her until the day he called at her hotel and found no trace of her or her belongings. At last the truth dawned, and Babbit hired a real detective to track her down. It took four years, but she was finally found—back home with her husband. She was convicted of swindling and sentenced to four years behind bars.

After only one year she was paroled, and proceeded to bilk a couple more wealthy victims, one of whom was that most ruthless and canny of businessmen, railroad magnate Jay Gould. The escapades earned her an even longer stretch in prison.

On her release, her husband took her back, steadfastly refusing to believe she had done anything wrong. Within two years, Mrs. Peck had flown the coop again. Posing as the wife of a Danish admiral, she took rooms at a fancy hotel and lived luxuriously on money she'd borrowed using the admiral's name and reputation. When bank investigators came to check up on her, she fled.

She went on to con an aged doctor out of his life savings, for which she was sentenced to five years in prison. When she got out, her long-suffering husband welcomed her back again with open arms—and again she made a fool of him by returning to New York City and her criminal career.

This time she managed to convince an elderly

Successful swindlers claim that the victims who are easiest to fool are those who are basically dishonest themselves. Jay Gould certainly fit the bill. He made much of his fortune by issuing illegal railroad stocks and bribing legislators.

diamond merchant that he should entrust her with twenty-one thousand dollars' worth of gems. She had no trouble finding a buyer for the stones, a man named Columbani. But instead of cash he paid her in negotiable bonds—which, Peck shortly discovered, he had recently stolen. Furious at having been conned herself, she contacted the police (without mentioning the diamonds, of course), who helped her set a trap for the thief.

When Columbani came around to buy more diamonds, he found the police waiting. He pulled a gun and might have shot his way out, except that Mrs. Peck coolly produced a pistol from her purse and plugged him in the hand. Columbani dived out the second-story window and crashed to the pavement, breaking several major bones.

Columbani's con inspired Mrs. Peck to devise a new scheme. The owner of a flourishing sign business agreed to sell stock in his company to Mrs. Peck and several accomplices, in exchange for an assortment of property deeds. What the owner didn't know was that the deeds were worthless forgeries. When Peck and her cronies had purchased so many shares that they controlled the company, they booted out the owner and proceeded to drain the business dry.

By this time Mrs. Peck was in her seventies, but showed no inclination to retire. Indeed, the fact that she was, to all appearances, just a "nice old lady" worked to her advantage. Finally, at seventy-nine, after swindling a prominent real estate company with more phony deeds, she was arrested again and sentenced to twenty years. In

The Victorian stereotype of women as innocent and helpless made it easier for female con artists, including Ellen Peck—photographed here in her late nineties—to dupe their male victims.

1909 she asked the governor for a pardon. He refused, insisting that "old age is no excuse for crime." Two years later his successor granted a full pardon and Mrs. Peck returned to her ever-faithful husband in time to celebrate their golden wedding anniversary.

If police thought they had seen the last of her, though, they were wrong. In 1913 a Latin American plantation owner filed a complaint against a charming woman who had sweet-talked him out of much of his land and money. The culprit was none other than Ellen Peck, now eighty-four. Detectives found her at her home, too ill to take into custody—but well enough to reply indignantly to their accusations, "How dare you? There is nothing in my life that is tainted. Gentlemen, you are looking at a devoted wife and a hard-working mother."

Four

The Yellow Kid

Ellen Peck's methods were very different from those of the typical con artist. She had plenty of charm and intelligence, two of a swindler's biggest assets. But her scams were rather direct and obvious—one reason she was caught and convicted so often.

Most successful con games are so subtle and complex that they often leave their victims unaware that they've been conned. Some are so intricate that it is nearly impossible to explain clearly how they work.

The majority of con games fall into one of two categories—the short con and the long con, or big con. As writer Luc Sante explains, "A short con involves taking the pigeon [victim] for all the money he has on his person, while the big con sends him home to get more."

Compared to the long con, which can require a good deal of time and a lot of accomplices, the typical short con is relatively quick and simple. But even the simplest scam demands a considerable amount of skill and finesse. For this reason, most of the great grifters learned the trade the same way Soapy Smith did—by working alongside a master.

It's possible to get a pretty complete picture of the history of con games by following the career of just one

Joseph "Yellow Kid" Weil seemed willing to cheat just about anyone, including his fellow cons. One colleague commented, "That Yellow Kid would tear himself off if he could."

man, Joseph Weil, who described himself as "the most successful and the most colorful confidence man that ever lived." It was not an empty boast. In a career that spanned half a century, Weil either originated, improved on, or participated in nearly all the classic cons, and in the process made an estimated eight million dollars.

Weil was born in 1877 in Chicago. He was, he later wrote, "a bright pupil" in school, "particularly good at mathematics." After school he was expected to work in his parents' grocery store. But Joseph preferred to spend his time at the local racetrack.

At seventeen he quit school and took a job with a collection agency. He soon learned that "by the use of my wits, I could earn more on the side than my regular salary." He had discovered that his fellow employees were keeping a percentage of the money they collected, and he offered to keep his mouth shut—for a price.

After two years he went to work for a "picturesque character" called Doc Meriwether, whose medicine show toured small Midwestern towns each summer. While his dancing girls attracted a crowd of men, Doc hawked bottles of Meriwether's Elixir, guaranteed to rid anyone of parasitic tapeworms—an extremely doubtful claim. The concoction did, however, have a profound effect on its users since it contained a dose of cascara, a powerful laxative. If sales were slow, Joseph, posing as a local boy, stepped forward to offer a glowing testimonial to the elixir's miraculous properties.

By the following summer he had devised a swindle of his own, using a technique that con artists call "the switch." First he gained the trust of the rural folk by offering a legitimate product—subscriptions to *Hearth and Home* magazine, then he switched to the scam. Producing a pair of gold-rimmed eyeglasses that he supposedly had found in the road, he expressed a desire to return them to their owner. More often than not his victim, eyeing the expensive-looking frames, offered him several dollars for the glasses. Though Weil made a show of reluctance, he was secretly delighted, for the rims weren't real gold. In fact Weil had paid only twenty-five cents for the spectacles, and had plenty more just like them.

According to Weil, this scheme and many others succeeded because of the universal human desire to get something for nothing. "All the people I swindled," he said, "had one thing in common—greed." Like most con men, he believed that people were "inherently dishonest and selfish," and used this belief to justify his own dishonesty.

When Weil returned to Chicago, he married a girl from a respectable, religious family. For a time he considered becoming a minister, but concluded that his low opinion of human nature would be a definite liability.

Unwilling to work at menial jobs—because of his frail health, he insisted—Weil hung around saloons and poolrooms, where his fondness for a comic strip titled "Hogan's Alley and the Yellow Kid" earned him his life-long nickname of the Yellow Kid. He also returned to his old haunt, the racetrack, which inspired several of his most ingenious cons.

Results of horse races were relayed to various betting locations around the city by Western Union. Weil convinced wealthy racing enthusiasts that he could tap into the telegraph wires, using a complicated-looking

Before he was officially banned from them, Weil spent most of his time at racetracks like this one in Chicago. He never bet on the horses, though; instead he offered "tips" to the other spectators—for a fee, of course—that supposedly helped them pick a winner.

"transformer." In this way, he claimed, he could intercept the actual results sent out by Western Union and, in their place, send phony results showing that whatever horse he had bet on was the winner. Victims who shelled out twelve thousand dollars for one of the "transformers" quickly learned to their dismay that the impressive device in fact did nothing at all.

He told other pigeons that his brother-in-law worked for Western Union, and he would give him race results before they went to the bookmakers. Armed with this information, he could place a bet on a horse that had already won. Victims were eager to get in on the scam, but somehow, instead of cleaning up, they always ended up being cleaned out.

Most of those he fleeced meekly accepted the loss. But one victim, a burly iceman, came back to the Yellow Kid's office seeking revenge. Weil's only escape route was up an elevator shaft. Clutching the greasy cables, he climbed nearly to the floor above before sliding back into the grasp of the iceman, who demanded his money back. Though Weil complied, the man beat him senseless anyway, to teach him a lesson.

It didn't work. Weil simply came up with a new scam. When racing authorities became aware of his swindles and banned him from the track, he moved on to new territory. After buying up a huge tract of worthless swampland at a dollar an acre, he divided it into small parcels, which he proceeded to give away, totally free. How did he make his money? Simple. He was in cahoots with the county recorder, who charged the considerable sum of thirty dollars to record the deeds for the lots, instead of the usual two dollars, and split the profit with Weil.

His wife continually begged him to go straight but, Weil said, "the notion that any swindler would be a great success if he turned to legitimate channels, is indeed erroneous." Thanks to his reputation, each time he tried to start a bona fide business, whether it was selling chewing gum or running a hotel, the police hassled him incessantly, assuming he was up to something crooked. Weil decided that making money dishonestly was a lot less trouble.

He also decided it was best to operate outside Chicago, where he wasn't so well known. At a hotel in Fort Wayne, Indiana, he pulled his most outrageous con. In talking to the hotel's owner, he "accidentally" revealed that he'd discovered a method for making flawless copies of money. As Weil had hoped, the man informed a friend, a prominent banker, who brought him a stack of thousand-dollar bills to be duplicated.

Weil dipped each bill into a solution of harmless chemicals, laid it atop a sheet of paper the same size, and placed the whole stack between two sheets of glass. Then he sealed the edges of the "money machine" with adhesive tape and instructed the banker not to touch it for eight hours—by which time Weil was far away, taking with him the fifty-seven thousand dollars. While the banker's attention had been elsewhere, he had substituted an identical "money machine" filled with blank paper.

In 1926 he made the mistake of buying $750,000 worth of negotiable bonds and reselling them, unaware that, like those bought by Ellen Peck, they were stolen property. Weil was arrested and sentenced to five years in a federal penitentiary. After his release, with police watching him more closely than ever, he headed for Europe.

On the ship was a beautiful, mysterious woman who called herself Viola Martin. Learning that she was actually the Comtesse de Paris, Weil arranged to meet her. As their friendship deepened, she reluctantly revealed that she was in desperate need of funds to release her brother, the Duke of Orléans, from political exile. Weil readily

In 1959 a magazine reported that Weil had died in 1934. The Yellow Kid, still alive and well at age 82, sued the magazine for libel.

loaned her ten thousand dollars, keeping her pearl neck-
lace as security.

But when the ship docked in London, the Comtesse
abruptly vanished. Both she and the pearls, it turned out,
were fakes. Weil mourned the loss of the lady more than
the loss of his money. "What a team we would have
made!" he wistfully commented.

In 1940 Weil was jailed again for mail fraud. When
he was freed, he "resolved that I would never again be
involved in anything that might send me to prison." The
Yellow Kid lived to the age of one hundred, but never
again pulled a swindle—at least none that police were
aware of. Instead, he worked as a telephone solicitor.

Though he had stolen millions of dollars in his
fifty-year career, he had thrown it all away on luxurious
living and bad investments. "It takes a great deal of bold-
ness, mixed with a vast amount of caution, to acquire a
fortune," he said. "But it takes ten times as much wit to
keep it."

Still, he never regretted his spendthrift ways, nor did
he show any remorse for his crimes. "People will tell you
that crime does not pay," he said. "But it paid me hand-
somely."

Five

The Greatest Faker

The Yellow Kid made the motivation for his cons sound simple and straightforward—"the desire to acquire money." But according to scholar Richard H. Blum, profit isn't always the main concern of swindlers. They may be more driven by a need to exercise power over others, thus "'proving' their cleverness and superiority." Certainly a desire for power seems to have been an important factor in the unsavory career of Gaston Means, labeled by FBI director J. Edgar Hoover "the greatest faker of them all." The United States attorney general called him simply a "human dog." Means himself boasted at one point that he had been accused of every major crime, including murder, and convicted of none.

Means was born in Concord, North Carolina, in 1879. When his father, a lawyer, was preparing a case for trial, he would send the boy into town, supposedly to buy candy but really to keep his ears open for useful gossip about the case or about the jurors.

Though Gaston showed no particular love of learning, he attended the University of North Carolina, then worked briefly as a schoolteacher. But his outgoing nature led him into a career as a traveling salesman for a cotton mill. He would undoubtedly have gone far except

Though he looks a bit dim-witted in this photograph, Gaston Means claimed to have "a brain of exceptional analytical power."

for one flaw: he was fond of posing as the owner's son. When word got back to the home office, he was fired.

Means didn't display any actual criminal tendencies, though, until the age of thirty-two. As he was riding in the sleeper car of a train, the chain supporting his bunk broke, and he landed on his head, fracturing his skull. Means sued the manufacturer for seventy-five thousand dollars, but collected only fourteen thousand. Though railroad authorities suspected that Means had deliberately caused the accident by cutting the chain, they couldn't prove it.

Whether or not the incident was one of Means's scams, it marked the beginning of his descent into deception. A reporter who had known Means in college believed that the head injury was responsible for the abrupt change in his old friend's behavior.

Means married in 1913 and a year later went to work for a New York detective agency. Though his boss, William J. Burns, called him "the most wonderful operator [I] ever knew," Means's methods were questionable, even criminal. He was assigned to protect Maude King, a Chicago millionaire's widow who was being fleeced by an English con artist. Means rescued her, only to begin systematically swindling her himself.

He kept Mrs. King a virtual prisoner in her apartment and secretly recorded all her conversations. Gradually he took control of her financial affairs. Within two years he had diverted a half million dollars of her money into his own bank account. Not content with that, Means "discovered" a forged will in which her deceased husband left her not the mere million in his original will, but his entire estate of six million dollars. When Mrs. King's lawyer got suspicious, Means whisked the widow off to North Carolina for a vacation—one that would prove fatal.

During a hunting trip, Means and Mrs. King became separated from the other members of their party. A little later Means came stumbling out of the woods with a tearful account of how Mrs. King had been toying with his pistol and it had gone off, killing her instantly.

Though the coroner declared the death accidental, police were skeptical, especially after investigating Means's mismanagement of Mrs. King's fortune. Then they found witnesses who had discussed a recent murder case with Means. According to them, Means had boasted that, if he had been the murderer, he would have lured the victim into the woods and arranged an apparent accident. But when Means was brought to trial in North Carolina, a jury of sympathetic men acquitted him and declared Mrs. King's death a suicide.

The outbreak of World War I provided Means with new opportunities for dirty dealing. The Germans hired him to deliver information about the American manufacture and delivery of weapons to Great Britain. At the same time he was being paid by the British to report on German espionage activity. When the United States entered the war, he added a third client—the U.S. Army Intelligence Service.

After the war William Burns was called to Washington, D.C., to head up the fledgling Bureau of

Investigation. Means joined him in 1921. The previous year, the Eighteenth Amendment to the Constitution had prohibited the production of alcohol by anyone except a few licensed distilleries. Means's main job at the bureau was arresting bootleggers—those who made or transported illegal liquor. He also, however, worked as a spy for President Warren G. Harding's wife, who suspected that her husband was cheating on her.

Though the bureau paid him a mere seven dollars a day, Means managed to rent an expensive house and hire three servants, plus a chauffeur who drove him around

Bureau of Investigation chief William J. Burns—shown here (with hand raised) being sworn in—was convinced that Means was a brilliant detective. But it seems likely that Means's supposed abilities at detection were just another con.

in a Cadillac. The source of his wealth was, of course, another scam. He had convinced bootleggers and other underworld figures that, because of his privileged position, he could obtain liquor licenses and arrange for federal criminal charges to be dropped—in return for a substantial bribe. He raked in so much money with his phony promises that he constructed a secret vault for it in his backyard— a hole twenty feet deep lined with clay pipe.

In 1922 Means resigned from the bureau but went on collecting bribes in exchange for protection he couldn't really provide. Finally several irate "clients" exposed him, and he was sentenced to four years in prison for larceny and conspiracy.

When he was released, Means, in need of money, collaborated with magazine writer May Dixon Thacker on a

Despite Means's claims, it's doubtful that Florence Harding did anything to contribute to her husband's death. Most historians agree that President Harding succumbed to a heart attack, possibly brought on by stress. Even so, rumors persist to this day that there was something mysterious about his demise.

book titled *The Strange Death of President Harding.* Harding had died of a heart attack in 1923, but Means claimed the president had been poisoned by his jealous wife.

Though the book was a runaway best-seller, Means didn't give up his other money-making schemes. He next offered his services, at a thousand dollars a week, to the wealthy Mrs. Finley Shepherd, head of an anticommunist group. Shepherd had received a letter, signed by "Agents from Moscow," that threatened her life, and she wanted Means to track down the killers—an impossible task, since they didn't exist. Means had composed the letter himself.

The kidnapping of aviator Charles Lindbergh's infant son in 1933 inspired Means's most nefarious fraud. He persuaded heiress Evalyn McLean, a close friend of the Lindberghs, that he could locate and return the kidnapped baby. McLean was well aware of Means's shady reputation. In fact she once called him "the best crook I had ever known." But she believed that, because of his connections to the underworld, he might have privileged information. When he told her that the kidnappers had contacted him and demanded a ransom of one hundred thousand dollars, she handed over the money.

Eventually authorities discovered that the boy had been murdered. Means wasn't a suspect, but he was arrested for fraud, despite his protests that he had returned the money to Mrs. McLean's lawyers. At his trial, Means changed his story; now he swore that he had delivered the ransom money, but the kidnappers

WANTED

INFORMATION AS TO THE WHEREABOUTS OF

CHAS. A. LINDBERGH, JR.

OF HOPEWELL, N. J.

SON OF COL. CHAS. A. LINDBERGH

World-Famous Aviator

This child was kidnaped from his home in Hopewell, N. J., between 8 and 10 p. m. on Tuesday, March 1, 1932.

DESCRIPTION:

Age, 20 months	Hair, blond, curly
Weight, 27 to 30 lbs.	Eyes, dark blue
Height, 29 inches	Complexion, light
Deep dimple in center of chin	
Dressed in one-piece coverall night suit	

ADDRESS ALL COMMUNICATIONS TO
COL. H. N. SCHWARZKOPF, TRENTON, N. J., or
COL. CHAS. A. LINDBERGH, HOPEWELL, N. J.

ALL COMMUNICATIONS WILL BE TREATED IN CONFIDENCE

COL. H. NORMAN SCHWARZKOPF
March 11, 1932   Supt. New Jersey State Police, Trenton, N. J.

The kidnapping and murder of Charles Lindbergh, Jr. was one of the most notorious crimes of the early twentieth century. German immigrant Bruno Hauptmann was convicted and executed, but later evidence suggested he may have been innocent.

hadn't turned over the baby. He also insisted that the body the Lindberghs had identified as their son was actually a substitute, planted by the kidnappers.

As he left the witness stand, he spotted J. Edgar Hoover. "How did you like that story?" he asked.

"I have never heard a wilder yarn," replied Hoover.

Grinning, the swindler said, "Well, it was a good story just the same."

Means was sentenced to fifteen years in Leavenworth. In 1938, still in prison, he died of a heart attack without revealing to anyone the whereabouts of Mrs. McLean's money.

Six

The True Con Artist

When historian Francis Russell called Gaston Means "a confidence man able to make his cheats and deceptions works of art," he was speaking figuratively. But there is a species of swindler whose deceptions are, literally, works of art.

Art forgery has a long and distinguished history. Early in their careers such renowned painters as Fra Filippo Lippi, Andrea del Sarto, and Sandro Botticelli boosted their reputations by faking the works of earlier masters. Even the youthful Michelangelo carved a statue of Cupid in the style of a previous century, aged it by burying it in the ground, then sold it to a collector as a genuine antique. Michelangelo's motive may not have been money, but rather a desire to put one over on the art experts of his day, who revered anything ancient and scorned anything new.

Four hundred years after Michelangelo's little fraud, the situation in the art world hadn't changed much. Critics were still lavishing praise on the old masters and largely ignoring contemporary artists. Bitter over the injustice of it, Dutch painter Hans van Meegeren was determined to make fools of the experts, whom he called "arrogant scum." He did it so cleverly that, even when he admitted his forgeries, no one would believe him.

Van Meegeren was born in the Netherlands in 1889. His small, frail body and poor health made him feel inferior to other children and, at the same time, instilled in him a fierce desire to succeed, to prove he was as good as anyone else, or better.

At first he planned to gain fame as an architect, and studied architecture at the Institute of Technology in Delft, the birthplace of the great seventeenth-century painter, Johannes (or Jan) Vermeer. Van Meegeren became so fascinated with Vermeer's work that he switched his emphasis from architecture to art. In 1912 he married and took a job teaching drawing and art history. In his spare time he worked hard at his own painting.

Though his pictures won a number of prizes, he had trouble finding buyers for them. One writer described them as "huge black-and-white compositions showing . . . torture scenes, skeletons, angry-looking soldiers"—not the sort of thing that was likely to appeal to the general public.

Frustrated, van Meegeren began producing pieces that were less experimental and more commercial. At the age of thirty-three he had his first major exhibition. The critics were unimpressed, even contemptuous. Van Meegeren was furious, even when he recalled the humiliation years later: "'No talent,' that's what they said about me! 'No imagination!' 'No personality!' I had to teach them a lesson; had to prove, once and for all, their utter incompetence."

One critic in particular galled him—a professor named Bredius, who practically worshiped Jan Vermeer. Van Meegeren concluded that the most satisfying way of getting revenge would be to forge a Vermeer, one good enough to fool Bredius and his colleagues and reveal "their shocking lack of knowledge and understanding."

Since only about thirty-five of Vermeer's paintings had survived, they were all well known. Van Meegeren decided his best bet, instead of copying an existing work, was to create a new, "undiscovered" one. Scientific methods of determining authenticity had improved considerably since William Henry Ireland's day. It wasn't enough just to paint something in Vermeer's style. The forgery had to convince experts that it had been painted in the seventeenth century.

The preparations alone took van Meegeren several years. First he purchased several minor paintings of the period and removed the paint from the canvas with a pumice stone. Then he set about collecting the same pigments Vermeer used, many of which were hard to come by. For an authentic crimson color he needed the dried bodies of an insect native to Mexico. To make blue he needed the rare and ridiculously expensive mineral lapis lazuli.

At last he began work on his masterpiece, staying locked in his studio so that not even his wife knew what he was up to. "It was the most thrilling, the most inspiring experience of my whole life!" van Meegeren recalled. "There were so many things to consider, so many traps to avoid. It took me about seven months—

seven months of constant solitude, of frantic labour, of unending delight!"

He titled the finished work, which portrayed Jesus and his disciples, *De Emmausganger* (known in English as *Christ at Emmaus*). To give it the impression of age, he baked the finished picture until the surface of the paint cracked slightly.

In 1937 van Meegeren passed the painting on to his lawyer. Claiming that he had found the canvas in the Paris apartment of a deceased Dutch businessman, the lawyer showed it to his client's old nemesis, Dr. Bredius. The critic confidently pronounced it "*the* masterpiece of Johannes Vermeer . . . quite different from all his other paintings and yet every inch a Vermeer." The Boymans Museum in Rotterdam eagerly bought it for 540,000 guilders—about $270,000.

Van Meegeren's ruse had succeeded far beyond his expectations—so well, in fact, that he knew the experts would simply dismiss him as a crank if he claimed to be the artist. So, instead of confessing, he proceeded to paint more phony Vermeers, plus some forgeries of Vermeer's contemporary, Pieter de Hooch, and sell them for fantastic sums. To explain his sudden leap in income, he claimed to have won the French lottery.

During World War II, a number of wealthy members of the German Nazi party became avid collectors of art, especially of the Dutch masters. But since the government of the Netherlands prohibited the export of any of its great paintings, it was up to van Meegeren to fill the demand. Hermann Goering, Hitler's second in command,

Hans van Meegeren claimed that, while he was creating fake Vermeers in his studio, the spirit of the real Vermeer kept him company. "I sensed his presence; he encouraged me. He liked what I was doing. Yes, he really did."

Though Jan Vermeer was known for his portraits and domestic scenes, and a few landscapes, art critics found nothing suspicious in the fact that the "newly discovered" Vermeers, such as Christ and the Adultress, *all featured religious subjects.*

paid just over a quarter of a million dollars for a false Vermeer called *Christ and the Adultress*.

After the war the painting was found among Goering's collection. Dutch authorities traced its sale back to van Meegeren and accused him of collaborating with the enemy by selling off their country's national treasures—a charge that could carry the death penalty. To save his skin, he revealed that *Christ and the Adultress* was not, in fact, a Vermeer at all, but a van Meegeren.

In this photo taken during his trial in 1947, van Meegeren sits in the box at left. The large painting on the wall at top center is his Vermeer-like Christ at Emmaus.

His claim was, of course, met with derision. Van Meegeren offered to prove it by creating another pseudo-masterpiece. He was allowed to return to his studio, where, under constant surveillance, he set about painting the Vermeer-like *Jesus in the Temple,* using the same materials and techniques as before.

Impressed, authorities subjected the other newly discovered Vermeers to chemical tests and X-ray analysis, and reluctantly concluded that they were fakes. Though the charge of treason was dropped, in November 1947 van Meegeren was convicted of fourteen counts of fraud and sentenced to a year in prison. He appealed to the queen for a pardon. But before she could reply, the frail forger died of a heart attack.

Since van Meegeren's death, his phony Vermeers have become almost as valuable as the real thing.

Seven
The Great Impostor

Like the phony Comtesse de Paris, who bilked Joseph Weil, most con artists are adept at assuming a fake identity when it suits their purpose. Weil himself frequently appropriated someone else's name and credentials in order to add credibility to one of his swindles. Around the turn of the twentieth century, Cassie Chadwick conned bankers into loaning her millions of dollars by posing as the daughter of steel tycoon Andrew Carnegie.

But for the con artist, imposture is only a temporary expedient, a tool for separating the victim from his money. The true impostor is after something more than mere money, or even power or revenge. What drives most impostors, according to the authors of *Crimes and Punishment*, is "a craving to *be* somebody, to be saluted and respected."

What other motive could account for someone like George Psalmanazar, who invented a fake alphabet, spoke in gibberish, and breakfasted on raw meat, all in order to convince eighteenth-century Londoners that he was a native of the mysterious island of Formosa? Or Louis de Rougemont, the Swiss butler who, two hundred years later, astounded the British again with tales of his thirty years as a "cannibal chief in the wilds of unexplored Australia"?

Fred Demara, the most famous and most accomplished impostor of all time, wasn't content to take just one alternate identity in his quest to "be somebody." He changed careers and credentials so often and so rapidly that even he admitted, "Sometimes it's hard to say what my name is."

His name was, in fact, Ferdinand Waldo Demara, Jr., and he was born in 1921 in the Massachusetts mill town of Lawrence. Though he was likable and outgoing, Fred was regarded with suspicion by the children of the mill-workers because his father, who owned a chain of movie theaters, was rich. The only way he could gain acceptance was by doing something bad or amusing. One of his pranks involved sticking two artificial legs into a snowbank to startle passing motorists.

When he was eleven, his father's business failed. The sudden poverty didn't make Fred fit in any better; it only made him feel humiliated. Fred was an impulsive boy; when he got a notion to do something, he seldom stopped to think about the consequences. When he was sixteen he made the first of many rash moves—he quit school and entered a Trappist monastery. Big and strong for his age, he didn't mind the hard work, but the diet—which didn't include meat, eggs, or fish—left him constantly hungry, and he had trouble keeping the vow of silence. Though he somehow lasted two years, the brothers concluded that he wasn't monk material.

Demara tried a less restrictive order, the Brothers of Charity, who assigned him to teach fourth grade at their school for boys. Without bothering to ask permission, he

Fred Demara's cheerful, outgoing personality helped him fit in anywhere. But his impostures took an emotional toll. "Every time I take a new identity," he said, "some part of the real me dies."

The textile mills of Lawrence, Massachusetts, attracted emigrants from all over Europe, making the city into a patchwork of ethnic neighborhoods. "Wherever I went in Lawrence, except on Jackson Street," Demara said, "I was always a stranger."

began taking his classes on field trips, and started a drive to collect toys and clothing for the boys. Instead of applauding his efforts, the brothers chastised him for acting without their approval.

Demara's pride was injured, and he did the same thing he would do time and again when things got tough—he bailed out. Though he'd never driven a car before, he stole the school's station wagon and took it to Boston, where he enlisted in the army. He quickly discovered that he wasn't cut out to be a soldier, either, and deserted.

Demara was normally a quick learner, but he didn't

learn much from his mistakes. Using a fake identity, he joined another monastery—only to be recognized by a brother who had known him during his first try at being a Trappist.

The United States had just entered World War II and, in a fit of patriotism, Demara enlisted in the navy. Though he trained as a medical corpsman, he was turned down for advanced medical school because of his lack of education. Demara determined to remedy that. With the help of stationery stolen from his commanding officer, he obtained grade transcripts and other credentials of a college graduate, then substituted his own name on the documents. The navy suddenly considered him a great candidate for officer school.

But Demara feared his background wouldn't stand up to a thorough check and decided it was time to disappear. He left behind a note implying that he had thrown himself into the ocean. "My only regret," he said, "was that I had but two or three lives to give for my country."

Incredibly, he returned to the Trappist monastery he'd fled from most recently. But this time he was posing as Dr. Robert Linton French. Unfortunately Dr. French was no better at self-denial than Fred Demara had been. He moved on. By the time he was twenty-four he had entered and been kicked out of a dozen different Catholic orders.

In 1945 "Dr. French" was hired by Gannon College in Erie, Pennsylvania, to head up their philosophy department. Demara successfully taught three different courses by reading up each night on the material he planned to cover the next day, thus keeping one day ahead of his students. But he still had a tendency to plunge into new projects without prior approval. When he was taken to task for it, he resigned on the spot.

His next position, at St. Martin's Abbey in Washington, ended quite differently. He was arrested by the FBI for deserting from the navy during wartime—an offense punishable by death. Demara felt that, to plead his case properly, he needed "a kind of honest liar. I was the exact man for the job." He somehow convinced the court that, as an innocent, idealistic boy fresh from a monastery, he had been compelled to desert in order to avoid being corrupted by his crude, foul-mouthed fellow seamen. He was sentenced to six years in prison but, thanks to good behavior, served only eighteen months.

The worst thing about the experience, he said, "was being Demara again . . . That guy was a bum." Posing as a biology professor, he joined the Brothers of Christian Instruction in Maine. There he met Dr. Joseph Cyr, a Canadian physician eager to get a license to practice in the United States. Demara borrowed all of the doctor's records, promising to present them to the Maine medical board. When, inevitably, he parted ways with the brothers, he enlisted in the Royal Canadian Navy, using Dr. Cyr's credentials.

While stationed in Halifax, Nova Scotia, he fell in love with a navy nurse. He didn't want to deceive her but he wasn't willing to reveal his true identity, either. He resolved the dilemma in his usual fashion: he left.

His new assignment was medical officer on the

destroyer *Cayuga*, which was headed for combat duty in Korea. The moment he stepped on board, he was rushed to the captain, who was in agony from a toothache. Demara locked himself in his cabin and desperately searched his medical manuals for help until the captain ordered him to come out. He shot the skipper full of novocaine and, wincing fearfully, yanked out a tooth that, fortunately, proved to be the infected one.

In Korea, the crew of the *Cayuga* took aboard nineteen wounded South Korean soldiers. One had a bullet near his heart, another a shell splinter in his groin, a third had a hole through one lung. Demara's brief stint as a medical corpsman hadn't begun to prepare him for this. But he knew that, without help, some of the men would surely die.

While the ship pitched wildly in a storm, he began operating. To his surprise, he seemed instinctively to know what to do, as though he'd been performing surgery for years, or as though he'd been a surgeon in a previous life. He worked all through the night. When he finally sewed up the last patient, the crew burst into cheers.

Demara went on to treat other soldiers and civilians in the area so successfully that his exploits were written up in newspapers back home, where they reached the notice of the real Dr. Cyr. Investigators dug up the phony doctor's past, and he was discharged from the navy.

In 1952, in need of money, Demara consented to an interview for *Life* magazine, a decision that would come back to haunt him. Still not content to be plain

Fred Demara, he borrowed the identity of a man named Ben W. Jones. Thanks to glowing recommendations that he composed himself, he landed a position at the maximum security prison in Huntsville, Texas.

Demara introduced several new and humane procedures, including the use of tranquilizers, and provided the inmates with movies, schooling, and reading material. Unfortunately, one of the magazines donated to the prison was a copy of *Life* magazine containing his interview. Not caring to become a prisoner at Huntsville himself, he took off again.

In an effort to escape his own reputation, Demara took a job at a tiny school near remote Point Barrow, Alaska. But a trapper came through who recalled the *Life* article and threatened to spill the beans unless Demara paid him off.

After one final imposture, teaching English, French, and Latin at a school in Massachusetts under the name Jefferson Baird Thorne, Demara seemed to resign himself to using his rightful identity. At first he had trouble finding anyone who would hire him, but eventually his notoriety faded. Just before his death in 1982 of heart failure, Demara was working as a chaplain at a hospital in Anaheim, California. By an odd coincidence, Dr. Joseph Cyr took a position at the same hospital. The doctor considered revealing the Great Impostor's past, but decided against it because Demara was, Cyr said, "doing a good job."

When you consider the distinguished alternate identities Demara always chose, it's pretty clear what he was

In 1960 Demara was hired to play nine minor roles in the motion picture The Hypnotic Eye. *On his arrival in Los Angeles, he faked out the studio personnel who were waiting to greet him, by posing as the plane's pilot.*

after—status and respect, without the bother of actually earning it. But when Demara himself was asked why he kept on posing as other people, he replied, "It's rascality, pure rascality."

GLOSSARY

Boswell, James (1740–1795)   Scottish writer best known for his 1791 biography *The Life of Samuel Johnson*.

Carnegie, Andrew (1835–1919)   American industrialist who donated much of his fortune to foundations, colleges, and libraries.

cascara   A thorny shrub of the American West Coast whose bark was once used as a cathartic, to clean out the digestive system.

Defoe, Daniel (1660–1731)   English journalist and fiction writer famous for his novel *Robinson Crusoe*, which he passed off as a factual account of an actual shipwrecked sailor.

Díaz, Porfirio (1830–1915)   A former general who became dictator of Mexico from 1876 until 1911, when his oppressive rule was ended by a revolution.

Formosa   An island off the coast of China, now known as Taiwan.

grifter   A small-time swindler.

Harding, Warren G. (1865–1923)   President of the United States from 1921 until his death. His administration was plagued by scandals, and historians believe that worry over them contributed to his fatal heart attack.

Hoover, J. Edgar (1895–1972)   Director of the Federal Bureau of Investigation for forty-eight years.

larceny   Theft, usually on a large scale.

Lindbergh, Charles (1902–1974)   American aviator who became a popular hero after his 1927 solo flight across the Atlantic Ocean.

Melville, Herman (1819–1891)   American author and poet whose best-known novel is the classic *Moby-Dick*.

Michelangelo (1475–1564)   Italian painter and sculptor whose frescoes on the ceiling of the Sistine Chapel in Rome are considered one of the world's greatest works of art.

monastery   The residence of a religious order, usually one whose members have taken vows of solitude and simplicity.

Mother Teresa (1910–1997)   Winner of the Nobel Peace Prize, founder of a Catholic order that aids the homeless and dying in India.

Nazi party   A German political party, led by Adolf Hitler, whose belief in the supremacy of the white race led to the deaths of millions of Jews and others during World War II.

petrified   Turned into stone by a process in which organic matter is displaced by dissolved minerals.

Sheridan, Richard Brinsley (1751–1816)   English playwright, politician, and theater manager, author of the play *The School for Scandal.*

tapeworm   A ribbonlike colony of worms that infests the intestines of humans and other animals. A colony can grow to over thirty feet in length.

travesty   A literary or artistic work that imitates a greater work, but does it so poorly that it seems to make fun of the original.

Vermeer, Jan (1632–1675)   Dutch painter whose sensitive portraits were largely overlooked by collectors and critics until nearly two hundred years after his death.

Walpole, Horace (1717–1797)   English author who originally claimed that his Gothic novel *The Castle of Otranto* was a true story, and that it was first published in Italy in the 1500s.

TO LEARN MORE ABOUT SWINDLERS

Books—*Nonfiction*

Streissguth, Thomas. *Hoaxes & Hustlers.* Profiles series. Minneapolis: Oliver Press, 1994.

A very readable history of con artists and their scams from the mid-nineteenth century to today.

Taggart, B., ed. *Big Book of Hoaxes.* New York: DC Comics, 1996.

A comprehensive, entertaining compendium of frauds and fallacies.

Books—*Fiction*

Beard, Darleen Bailey. *The Flimflam Man.* New York: Farrar, Straus, 1998.

In the 1950s, a swindler sells tickets for a nonexistent circus to the residents of ten-year-old Bobbie Jo Hailey's hometown of Wetumka, Oklahoma. Based on a real incident (see Festivals below).

Paulsen, Gary. *Dunc and the Scam Artists.* New York: Yearling, 1993.

During a ski trip to Colorado, Dunc and his best friend Amos uncover a con game that preys on the town's elderly citizens.

On-line Information*

www.syntac.net/hoax

An interesting, colorfully written and illustrated site that offers a wealth of capsule comments and longer stories about forgers, hoaxers, con artists, and frauds of all kinds, plus links to related sites.

Websites change from time to time. For additional on-line information, check with the media specialist at your local library.

Movies

The Sting, directed by George Roy Hill. Starring Paul Newman and Robert Redford.

This 1973 film, which won Oscars for Best Picture and Best Screenplay, is great fun—fast-paced, well acted, and full of surprises. It also accurately portrays various con games in vogue during the early twentieth century, including an incredibly complex racing-related long con that is nearly identical to those devised by the Yellow Kid. Available for rental at video stores.

Festivals

Sucker Days, Wetumka, Oklahoma. Chamber of Commerce, 202 North Main

Street, Wetumka, OK 74883-3009. 1-405-452-3237.
This annual celebration, held in the third week of August, commemorates the fleecing of the town in 1950 by a traveling con artist.

BIBLIOGRAPHY

American Heritage Magazine. *Stories of Great Crimes & Trials*. New York: American Heritage, 1974.

Anthony, Carl Sferrazza. *Florence Harding: The First Lady, the Jazz Age, and the Death of America's Most Scandalous President*. New York: Morrow, 1998.

The Associated Press. "Federal investigation targets ring selling fake memorabilia." *The Carthage (MO) Press*, April 12, 2000.

Berton, Pierre. *The Klondike Fever: The Life and Death of the Last Great Gold Rush*. New York: Knopf, 1958.

Blum, Richard H. *Deceivers and Deceived: Observations on Confidence Men and Their Victims, Informants and Their Quarry, Political and Industrial Spies and Ordinary Citizens*. Springfield, IL: Charles C. Thomas, 1972.

Blundell, Nigel. *The World's Greatest Crooks and Conmen*. New York: Berkley, 1991.

Brannon, W. T. *The Con Game and "Yellow Kid" Weil: The Autobiography of the Famous Con Artist as Told to W. T. Brannon*. New York: Dover, 1974.

Crichton, Robert. *The Great Impostor*. New York: Random House, 1959.

Crimes and Punishment: The Illustrated Crime Encyclopedia. Westport, CT: H. S. Stuttman, 1994.

De Grave, Kathleen. *Swindler, Spy, Rebel: The Confidence Woman in Nineteenth-Century America*. Columbia, MO: University of Missouri, 1995.

Dornstein, Ken. *Accidentally, on Purpose: The Making of a Personal Injury Underworld in America*. New York: St. Martin's, 1996.

Dorset, Phyllis Flanders. *The New Eldorado: The Story of Colorado's Gold and Silver Rushes*. New York: Macmillan, 1970.

Editors of Time-Life Books. *Hoaxes and Deceptions*. Alexandria, VA: Time-Life, 1991.

Hancock, Ralph, with Henry Chaftez. *The Compleat Swindler*. New York: Macmillan, 1968.

Klein, Alexander, ed. *Grand Deception: The World's Most Spectacular and Successful Hoaxes, Impostures, Ruses and Frauds*. London: Faber and Faber, 1956.

MacAdam, Pat. *"The Great Impostor's last victim"* on www.ottawacitizen.com

McCormick, Donald. *Taken For a Ride: The History of Cons and Con-men.* London: Harwood-Smart, 1976.

MacDougall, Curtis D. *Hoaxes.* New York: Dover, 1958.

Mackay, Charles, LL.D. *Extraordinary Popular Delusions and the Madness of Crowds.* New York: Harmony, 1980.

Mann, Thomas. *Stories of Three Decades.* Translated by H. T. Lowe-Porter. New York: Modern Library, 1936.

Maurer, David W. *The American Confidence Man.* Springfield, IL: Charles C. Thomas, 1974.

Maurer, David W. *The Big Con: The Story of the Confidence Man.* New York: Doubleday, 1999.

Melville, Herman. *Pierre, Israel Potter, The Piazza Tales, The Confidence-Man, Uncollected Prose, Billy Budd, Sailor.* New York: Library of America, 1984.

Moger, Art, ed. *Pros and Cons.* Greenwich, CT: Fawcett, 1975.

Nash, Jay Robert. *Hustlers & Con Men.* New York: M. Evans, 1976.

Phelan, James. *Scandals, Scamps and Scoundrels: The Casebook of an Investigative Reporter.* New York: Random House, 1982.

Prassel, Frank Richard. *The Great American Outlaw: A Legacy of Fact and Fiction.* Norman, OK: University of Oklahoma, 1993.

Russell, Francis. *The Shadow of Blooming Grove: Warren G. Harding in His Times.* New York: McGraw-Hill, 1968.

Sifakis, Carl. *Hoaxes and Scams: A Compendium of Deceptions, Ruses and Swindles.* New York: Facts on File, 1993.

Symons, Julian. *A Pictorial History of Crime.* New York: Crown, 1966.

Whitehead, John. *This Solemn Mockery: The Art of Literary Forgery.* London: Arlington, 1973.

INDEX

Page numbers for illustrations are in boldface

accomplices, 32
Army, U.S., 44, 60
art forgery, 49–52, **53**, **54**, 55–56, **55**
authenticity, techniques used for, 11, 56

Babbit, B. T., 26–27
Berton, Pierre, 23
Blonger brothers, 21
Blum, Richard H., 41
bootleggers, 45, 46
Boswell, James, 13–14
Botticelli, Sandro, 49
Bredius, Dr., 51, 52
bribes, 46
Bureau of Investigation, 44–45, 46
Burns, William J., 43, 44–45, **45**

Carnegie, Andrew, 57
cascara, 34
Cayuga (destroyer), 63
Chadwick, Cassie, 57
Chatterton, Thomas, 11, 13, 19
Columbani (con man), 29
Committee 101, 22, 23
Committee of Law and Order, 22
Comtesse de Paris, 38, 40, 57
con games, 33–38, **33**, **39**, 40
    long con/big con, 32
    short con, 32
confidence artists (con artists), 6, 8, 17–24, **19**,

24, 25, 33–38, **33**, **39**, 40
    confidence women, 25–31, **30**
Confidence Man, The (Melville), 8
confidence trick, 8
Cyr, Joseph, 62, 63, 64

Defoe, Daniel, 9
Demara, Fred, 58, **59**, 60–65, **65**
Denver, Colorado, 18, 20, 21, **21**
Díaz, Porfirio, 20

Eighteenth Amendment, 45
Elizabeth I, 14
espionage, 44

fakery, 6, 7, 41, **42**, 43–48
Ford, Bob, 20
forgeries, 6, 7
    art, 49–52, **53**, **54**, 55–56, **55**
    literary forgers, 9, **10**, 11–16, **12**, **16**
Formosa, 57
Franklin, Benjamin, 9
fraud, 6

gambling hall, 21
Goering, Hermann, 52, 55
goldfields, 21, 22, 23
Gould, Jay, 27, **28**
grifters, 18, 25, 32

Hancock, Ralph, 6
Harding, Florence, 45, **46**,

47
Harding, Warren G., 45, 47
Hathaway, Anne, 13, 14
Hauptmann, Bruno, 48
Hooch, Pieter de, 52
Hoover, J. Edgar, 41, 48
horse racing scam, 35–37, **36**

impostors, 6–7, 57–58, **59**, 60–65, **65**
Ireland, Samuel, 11, 12–13, 15
Ireland, William Henry, 11–16, **12**, 51

James Gang, 20
James, Jesse, 20
Journal of the Plague Year, A, 9

Kemble, John, 15
King, Maude, 43–44
Korea, 63

Lawrence, Massachusetts, 58, **60**
Life magazine, 63–64
Lincoln, Abraham, 6
Lindbergh, Charles, Jr., 47–48, **48**
Lippi, Fra Filippo, 49
literary forgers, 9, **10**, 11–16, **12**, **16**

McGwire, Mark, 6
McLean, Evalyn, 47, 48
Means, Gaston, 41, **42**, 43–48, 49

Melville, Herman, 8
Meriwether, Doc, 34
Michelangelo, 49
monasteries, 58, 60, 61, 62
money machine scam, 38
Mother Teresa, 6

Navy, U.S., 61, 62
Nazi party, 52

Onomacritus (Father of Fakers), 7
Operation Bullpen, 6

Peck, Ellen, 25–31, **30**, 32, 38
Peck, Richard W., 26
pigeons (victims), 32, 36
Poe, Edgar Allen, 11
Prohibition, 45
protection scam, 46
Psalmanazar, George, 57

Reid, Frank, 23–24

Riley, James Whitcomb, 9, 11
Rougemont, Louis de, 57
Rowley, Thomas, 11
Royal Canadian Navy, 62
Russell, Francis, 49

Sante, Luc, 32
Sarto, Andrea del, 49
Shakespeare scam, 12–16, **16**
Shakespeare, William, 12–13
shell game, 8, 18
Shepherd, Mrs. Finley, 47
Sheridan, Richard Brinsley, 14, 15
Skagway, Alaska, 22
Smith, Jefferson Randolph (Soapy Smith), 17–24, **19**, 32
Soap Gang, 18–19, 22
switch technique, the, 34–35

Thacker, May Dixon, 46–47
Thimbleriggers, 18, 24

Van Meegeren, Hans, 49–52, **53**, **55**, 56
Vermeer, Johannes, 51, 52, **54**, 55, 59
vigilantes, 22, 23, 25
Volunteers, the (vigilante group), 25

Walpole, Horace, 11
Weil, Joseph (The Yellow Kid), 25, 33–38, **33**, **39**, 40, 41, 57
Western Union, 35–36
Whitehead, John, 9
women, confidence, 25–31, **30**
World War I, 44
World War II, 52, 55, 61